SEVERN VALLEY
R·A·I·L·W·A·Y

Visitor Guide

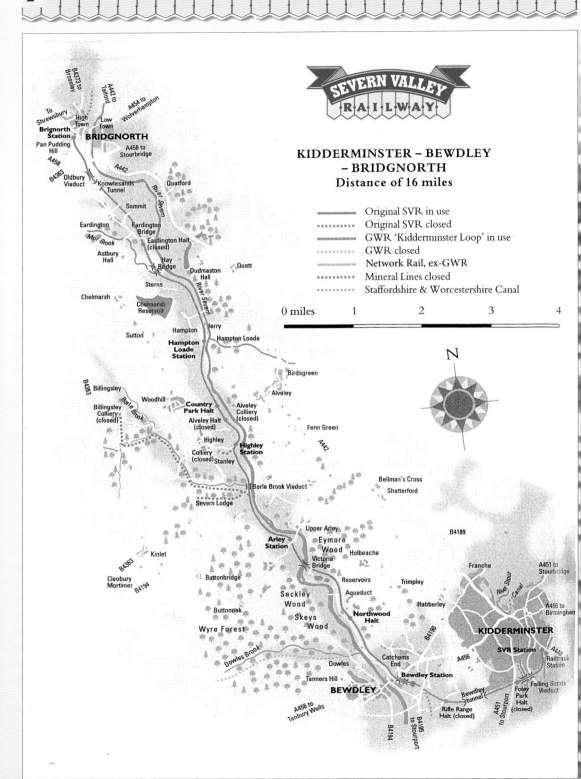

SEVERN VALLEY RAILWAY

KIDDERMINSTER – BEWDLEY – BRIDGNORTH
Distance of 16 miles

Original SVR in use
Original SVR closed
GWR 'Kidderminster Loop' in use
GWR closed
Network Rail, ex-GWR
Mineral Lines closed
Staffordshire & Worcestershire Canal

0 miles 1 2 3 4

N

A wave to the driver at historic Bewdley station.

This is a typical Severn Valley Railway experience; a train of the 1930s is perfectly recreated eighty years later! GWR 'small Prairie tank No 4566 and a train of matching coaches crosses the picturesque Oldbury viaduct near Bridgnorth on 8 October 2015. *Matthew Toms*

Walking down the train corridor to find a comfortable compartment seat.

A close up view of a 124 ton steam locomotive is possible at Highley Engine House.

December each year means a train journey to Arley to visit Santa's grotto.

One of the highlights of a train journey along the Severn Valley is the crossing of the River Severn by means of the 1861-built Victoria Bridge, south of Arley. Here is GWR 4-6-0 No 7802 *Bradley Manor* heading a southbound train from Bridgnorth to Kidderminster on 30 September 2016. *Alan Corfield*

AUTUMN IN THE VALLEY: LMR Ivatt Class 4 2-6-0 No 43106 leaves Hampton Loade alongside the River Severn with a Bridgnorth to Kidderminster train on 27 October 2012. *Alan Corfield*

About the Severn Valley Railway

During the past fifty years, the Severn Valley Railway has progressively achieved great prominence in British railway preservation. Nowadays, the initials 'SVR' are understood not only by keen railway enthusiasts, who still come in large numbers to our special gala events, but by the general public who have travelled on the line since 1970. This, in no small way, is due to extensive media coverage which has ensured that very few days pass without Severn Valley steam trains appearing in the press or on television screens across the Midlands, and indeed Britain.

WHAT IS IT?

What exactly is the Severn Valley Railway? It is a full-sized standard-gauge line running regular steam-hauled passenger trains, used by visitors, tourists and enthusiasts alike, between Kidderminster in Worcestershire and Bridgnorth in Shropshire, a distance of 16 miles. The journey is certainly an interesting one, for the Railway closely follows course of the River Severn for most of its route. The highlight of the trip is the crossing of the River Severn by means of Victoria Bridge, a massive 200-foot single span high above the water. There being few roads in the valley, most of the scenery can only be viewed by the Railway's

passengers; the landscape is quite varied and largely unspoilt, being punctuated only by the 'olde worlde' charm of several stations, each one giving ready access to local villages and riverside walks.

WHEN?

Train services operate at weekends from late February until the end of November, and daily during local school holiday periods and also from early May to late September. Services generally run from 10 a.m. until late afternoon at a frequency to suit passenger demand, and the single journey between Kidderminster and Bridgnorth takes just over one hour.

Passengers on the Railway may break the journey at any station and join a later train if they so desire. Passengers holding full-length return tickets may make as many journeys as they wish during normal operating days, and on gala days when special 'Rover' tickets are available, giving unlimited travel on a more intensive service of trains. First and Third class tickets are available, reflecting rail travel as it was until the 1960s. Except at certain events, young people aged 4 to 15 inclusive travel at child rate and children under four travel free. Family tickets are also available.

SPECIAL EVENTS

Santa specials are operated during December weekends, usually over the southern part of the line from Kidderminster to Arley, with Festive Season specials running from Boxing Day until the New Year, usually over the whole length of the line. There are popular Family Fun events during the year. One of the green diesel multiple-unit trains is used on 'Evening Cruises' on certain Saturdays in the summer. And main-line diesel locomotives operate passenger trains within the steam service, also during summer Saturdays and certain other days.

FACILITIES

Catering facilities are available at Kidderminster, Bewdley and Bridgnorth stations, and there are sales shops and real ale bars at Bridgnorth and Kidderminster. Refreshments are provided on most Severn Valley trains, with a full meal service on the 'Severn Valley Limited' and 'Severn Valley Venturer' trains on Sundays and certain other occasions – please note that advance booking is essential to dine on these trains.

Special trains may be hired throughout the year; details of these and other facilities, also general information about the Railway including the annual timetable, can be obtained from the Severn Valley Railway, Number One, Comberton Place, Kidderminster, DY10 1QR.

Car parking is usually available at Kidderminster, Bewdley and Bridgnorth stations; the additional field parking area at Bridgnorth is also in use from April to October.

Kidderminster Town SVR station is adjacent to the Network Rail one, currently served by West Midlands and Chiltern trains. Bridgnorth SVR station is 13 miles from Wolverhampton Network Rail station, linked by a bus service at certain times. Here West Midlands, Cross Country and Virgin services are to be found.

For safety reasons, it is regretted that admission to SVR repair workshops can only be permitted on special occasions, or by prior arrangement.

STAFFING

An important feature of the Railway not readily appreciated by visitors is that it is very largely operated by unpaid volunteers, paid staff being responsible for some administrative and commercial activities, plus track and rolling stock maintenance. Throughout the year, several hundred volunteers visit the Railway to perform a variety of tasks, including repairing and repainting stations, locomotives and rolling stock; many of the trades involved require training and this is provided by professionals who give their time freely. The volunteer atmosphere is friendly, and more people are always needed, the main stipulation being that all workers must be Severn Valley Railway Company members for insurance purposes. Details of how to join are given on page 68.

No description of the Railway would be complete without a mention of the Railway's own visitor centre, The Engine House at Highley, very near to the station. Locomotives, rolling stock and railwayana are on display, with film presentations, observation galleries, a restaurant and a gift shop, not forgetting a play area for children.

THE CHARM OF COUNTRY STATIONS: S.R. 'Battle of Britain' 4-6-2 No 34053 'Sir Keith Park' arrives at Highley to a busy platform on 13 September 2012. The train is southbound from Bridgnorth to Kidderminster. The Engine House visitor centre is a short walk away from here. *John Oates*

Time Line

A brief history of the Severn Valley Line

1853 Parliamentary authority obtained to build the Severn Valley Railway from Hartlebury to Shrewsbury.

1858-61 Railway constructed.

1862 Severn Valley line opened to passengers as part of the West Midland Railway.

1872 Severn Valley line fully absorbed into the Great Western Railway.

1878 Great Western Railway opened 'The Loop' from Bewdley to Kidderminster.

1940-1 Severn Valley line at its busiest during the Second World War.

1948 Upon nationalisation, the Great Western Railway became British Railways Western Region.

1950 Diesel railcars appeared on certain services.

1963 Severn Valley line closed to all through traffic between Alveley and Shrewsbury.

1965 Preservation scheme launched at Kidderminster meeting. Severn Valley Railway Society established headquarters at Bridgnorth.

1969 Alveley Colliery closed, thus the line south to Bewdley became disused.

1970 BR passenger services from Bewdley to Kidderminster and Hartlebury ceased. SVR passenger services from Bridgnorth to Hampton Loade commenced.

1974 SVR passenger services extended, first to Highley, then to Bewdley.

1982 Foley Park sugar factory closed, thus the line to Kidderminster became disused.

1984 SVR passenger services extended to Kidderminster; line now 16 miles long.

2007 SVR between Bewdley and Bridgnorth ravaged by The Great Storm, line damaged in 45 places. Kidderminster to Bewdley was unaffected.

2008 After nine months out of use and nearly £3 million spent on repairs, Bewdley to Bridgnorth reopened.

2015 SVR celebrated **fifty years** of the preservation scheme with special events.

2016 Kidderminster Diesel Maintenance Depot opened.

The first Severn Valley Railway Company was truly in the transport business as a through secondary route from Hartlebury to Shrewsbury within the national network for the 101 years from 1862 until 1963. Today's Severn Valley Railway is principally in the leisure business, commencing operations in 1970 from Bridgnorth to Hampton Loade, extending services southwards to Bewdley in 1974, then to Kidderminster in 1984. Here is the story in a little more detail...

THE FIRST SEVERN VALLEY RAILWAY COMPANY

The idea of building a railway along the Severn valley from Shrewsbury to Worcester was first mooted in 1846, but several proposals were considered before Royal Assent (parliamentary authority) was given to the Severn Valley Railway Bill of 1853. This document provided for the village of Hartlebury, near Droitwich in Worcestershire, on the Oxford, Worcester & Wolverhampton (later West Midland) Railway, to be linked by 40¾ miles of railway to Shrewsbury, county town of Shropshire, and already an important railway route focus.

The Severn Valley line was never a particularly busy passenger line before preservation, and this short train was typical. Recorded at Arley in 1932, 0-4-2 tank No 1440 and auto-coach No 39 are working from Bridgnorth or Highley to Bewdley. The historic station building survives in full use today, to the delight of visitors. *Selwyn Higgins*

Left: For more than 50 years 0-6-0 tender locomotives like this one worked most of the freight trains and some of the passenger trains on the Severn Valley line. Here is Dean Goods '2301' Class No 2339 of Worcester heading north from Bridgnorth for Shrewsbury in 1938.
Ian Button

The construction contract for the line was awarded to the prestigious railway building consortium of Messrs Brassey, Peto and Betts, with John (later Sir John) Fowler as Engineer-in-Chief and Henry Orlando Bridgman as Resident Engineer. Despite geological and financial problems, construction proceeded rapidly and was accomplished during the three years from 1858 until 1861.

The railway opened to much celebration by local people, particularly the invited guests, on Friday 31 January 1862. The opening to the wider public for through passenger and goods services occurred on the next day, Saturday 1 February. The route placed the important communities of Stourport-on-Severn, Bewdley, Bridgnorth and Ironbridge on the railway map for the first time. Only Coalport had been reached by rail previously, when it became the terminus of a branch line opened by the London & North Western Railway one year earlier in 1861.

From the outset, the Severn Valley Railway never owned its own locomotives or rolling stock, these being hired from the West Midland Railway (WMR). This Company had itself only recently (1860) been formed by the amalgamation of the Oxford, Worcester & Wolverhampton Railway and the Worcester & Hereford Railway. Also in 1860, the WMR became part of the Great Western Railway. Although regarded as independent in certain respects, the Severn Valley Railway was actually in the thrall of the West Midland Railway for financial support during its first decade. Indeed, the first Severn Valley line timetable for 1862 was headed 'West Midland Railway'.

THE GREAT WESTERN RAILWAY TAKEOVER

The mid-19th century was a period of many railway amalgamations and absorptions, and unsurprisingly it was only a short time – 1872 in fact – before the Severn Valley Railway was completely absorbed into the huge Great Western Railway empire.

The early railway network in this part of the Severn valley was augmented by three further lines, the Bewdley to Tenbury Wells (Wyre Forest) line of 1864, the Wellington to Buildwas (Coalbrookdale) line, also completed in 1864, and the Buildwas to Much Wenlock line of 1862, extended to Craven Arms in 1867 (the Wenlock Railway). The last two lines formed a rail link that crossed the Severn Valley line at Buildwas, near Ironbridge. All of these routes increased the patronage on the Severn Valley line, and all eventually came under Great Western Railway ownership.

Typical steam locomotive types seen on the Severn Valley line from the late 1920s to the early 1960s were GWR 0-6-0 pannier tank and small 2-6-2 side tank types (small 'Prairies').

Right: '4575' Class No 5538 of Shrewsbury is northbound at Linley Halt, the next stop north of Bridgnorth, in 1961.
Phil Coutanche

The final link in the local rail network was supplied by the Great Western Railway itself. This was the long-planned Bewdley to Kidderminster 'loop line', construction of which started in 1874. The opening, with little ceremony, occurred on Saturday 1 June 1878. Usefully, it enabled Severn Valley trains to run directly to and from Kidderminster (for Birmingham or Wolverhampton) as an alternative to the original SVR route to and from Hartlebury (for Worcester). In practice, the 'loop line' was used more frequently by trains to and from the Wyre Forest line. Kidderminster had been rail-served since 1852

Several more rail routes were projected, but only one, the Bridgnorth to Wombourne scheme (for direct access to Wolverhampton), ever reached the advanced planning stage.

Above: '5700' Class pannier tank No 9657 of Shrewsbury is southbound at Jackfield Crossing in the historic Ironbridge gorge. *D. Fereday Glenn*

Below: The GWR large 2-6-2 side tanks (large 'Prairies') appeared from the 1940s. '5101'Class No 5153 of Kidderminster is heading the Shrewsbury Coton Hill to Kidderminster goods train at Cressage on 2 March 1963 *Roger Sellick*

TRAIN SERVICES ALONG THE VALLEY BEFORE PRESERVATION

GREAT WESTERN DAYS

Although providing an essential service within the area for just over 101 years, the Severn Valley line was never financially sound, and during West Midland Railway and Great Western Railway ownership the pattern and frequency of passenger services remained broadly the same, despite local calls from time to time for service improvements. The timetable soon settled down to feature four trains in each direction daily from Mondays to Saturdays, all travelling along the whole length of the line, two during the morning and two in the afternoon/early evening. Also, there were a few short workings on the southern end of the line for miners and other workers, and one return trip to Bridgnorth on Sundays in the summer for fishermen and day-trippers. On Bank Holidays a Birmingham Snow Hill to Bewdley scheduled service could sometimes be extended to Shrewsbury. Outside the normal timetable there were summer day excursions for visitors from a wide area of the Midlands to Bewdley and usually to Stourport, but occasionally to Bridgnorth. Conversely, residents in the Severn Valley were served by day excursions to seaside resorts.

Goods traffic, mostly of an agricultural or domestic nature, and coal trains from Alveley Colliery, Highley, to the power stations at Buildwas (opened in 1932) and Stourport (rail-connected in 1940) were the principal sources of revenue on the line. Indeed, Alveley coal could only be transported away in bulk by rail, owing to the lack of suitable roads in the area.

The gradual introduction of road motor vans and lorries in the late 1930s started the decline in rail goods services. The line was at its busiest briefly during the Second World War, when extra traffic was generated by the opening of RAF Bridgnorth and other military installations in the area. Also, the rural surroundings of the line ensured its suitability for long-distance trains to be diverted to avoid the busy West Midlands industrial area, which was highly vulnerable to enemy air attack during the Blitz of 1940 and 1941.

Diesel railcars started to replace steam trains on the Severn Valley line, particularly south of Bridgnorth, in the 1950s. The very successful GWR single units were the first, and here is an unidentified Swindon-built 'razor-edge' car powered by two AEC bus-type engines, southbound at Hampton Loade in 1959.
W. A. Camwell

BRITISH RAILWAYS DAYS, AND CLOSURE

Nationalisation of the British railway network on 1 January 1948 placed the Severn Valley line in the ownership of the Western Region of the newly formed British Railways, but brought no perceptible changes to its services. However, very soon into the 1950s the gradual post-war economic recovery of Britain saw the widespread increase in ownership of family motor cars, and a corresponding decline in rural railway passenger traffic.

Certain economies were made in this period, particularly the increased use of GWR single-unit diesel railcars on services mostly south of Bridgnorth during the late 1940s and 1950s, and BR single and multiple unit diesel trains at the end of the decade. Nevertheless, a few steam-hauled trains survived to the last days of the line, mainly operating north of Bridgnorth.

BR regional boundary changes saw lines in the Severn valley area under London Midland Region control on 1 January 1963. The Severn Valley line itself was closed as a through route between Bewdley and Shrewsbury later that year. Ordinary passenger trains ceased to run after Saturday 7 September 1963 (except for a steam-hauled fishermen's special from Birmingham Snow Hill via Bewdley to Bridgnorth and back as a finale on the following day). Through goods services last ran on Saturday 30 November 1963.

The disused track from the north into Bridgnorth was removed in rail-length panels during a BR demolition programme in early 1965. The best panels recovered between Much Wenlock, Buildwas and Bridgnorth were re-used

in the sidings of the Bescot (Walsall) marshalling yard, which were being extended at the time.

To the south, coal trains continued to operate from Alveley Colliery, near Highley, to Stourport power station until the colliery closed on Friday 31 January 1969, the surplus coal stocks being cleared by the end of March. During the same period, passenger trains continued to link Bewdley with Hartlebury and Kidderminster until Saturday 3 January 1970.

After the closure of Alveley Colliery, Granville Colliery in Shropshire and Littleton Colliery in Staffordshire were contracted to supply coal to Stourport power station by rail over the

British Railways Standard design 3MT 2-6-2 tanks appeared in the 1950s. No 82005 of Machynlleth is seen at Arley with the afternoon Shrewsbury to Kidderminster train on 25 May 1963. All 45 of these locos were scrapped in the 1960s, but a new one, No 82045, is currently being built at Bridgnorth. *Brian Moone*

The final type of diesel railcar used on the Severn Valley line in BR days was the Gloucester RCW single unit, sometimes augmented by a trailer car. Here, car No W55006 calls at Jackfield Halt with a Kidderminster to Shrewsbury service on 8 October 1962. *Roger Sellick*

remaining 2¾ miles of the Severn Valley line from Hartlebury to Stourport until Friday 30 March 1979, although this section was not officially closed until Monday 12 January 1981, while nuclear power options at Stourport were examined. The British Sugar Corporation terminated its contract to send rail traffic over the 1½-mile section from Kidderminster to Foley Park after Friday 22 January 1982, and thus all BR operations at the southern end of the Severn Valley system ceased completely.

This sequence of closures could have signalled the end of the Severn Valley Railway story, but preservation progress was neatly able to match much of the BR retreat...

THE PRESERVATION ERA

Severn Valley line preservation dates from Sunday 6 July 1965, when a group of railway enthusiasts led by Keith Beddoes formed the Severn Valley Railway Society at Kidderminster. Initial efforts by an expanding group of people succeeded in raising the 10 per cent deposit of the required £25,000 purchase price for the then disused 5½-mile section of the Severn Valley line from Bridgnorth through Hampton Loade to Alveley. Alveley was chosen to maintain the connection with the British Railways system, because Alveley Colliery was still open at that time, sending coal traffic southwards.

On Saturday 25 March 1967 the first rolling stock, an engine and four

coaches, arrived at Bridgnorth. The first years were spent in restoring the line to operating condition, and obtaining the legal authority, a Light Railway Order, from the then Department of the Environment. The 4½-mile section from Bridgnorth to Hampton Loade was opened for public passenger services on Saturday 23 May 1970, and the remainder of the purchase price was paid shortly afterwards.

Following closure of Alveley Colliery early in 1969, and cessation of all Bewdley passenger services early in 1970, a share issue was launched in 1973. This was to raise a further £110,000, of which £74,000 was to be spent on purchasing the disused 9 miles of railway from Alveley throug:

Scene of dereliction: Bridgnorth station on 24 April 1966, in the very early days of the Severn Valley Railway Society. 'Rolling stock' was limited to a 4-wheeled push trolley. *David C. Williams.*

The first train in preservation leaves Bridgnorth for Hampton Loade on Saturday 23 May 1970, powered by GWR Collett Goods '2251' Class 0-6-0 loco No 3205, the only survivor of a locomotive type used on the line in GWR and BR days. *SVR Archive*

Highley, Arley and Bewdley to Foley Park, near Kidderminster. The Bewdley to Foley Park section was purchased at that time to again maintain the connection with the British Rail network, which was still operating to Foley Park from Kidderminster with British Sugar Corporation traffic.

Spearheaded by the late Sir Gerald Nabarro, the share issue was so successful that it was oversubscribed, but the line itself was only reopened after a further financial contribution plus engineering expertise from the Rubery Owen Group of Companies and much practical work by volunteers. The train service was extended, firstly over the 2 miles from Hampton Loade to Highley on Good Friday 12 April 1974, then the further 6 miles from Highley through Arley to Bewdley on Saturday 18 May of that year.

The 2-mile section from Bewdley to Foley Park, though bought by the SVR as part of the package in 1973, was not used until 1980, and then only on special occasions. These included SVR steam trains from Bridgnorth during Enthusiast Weekends from 11 September 1976, BR diesel multiple units from Kidderminster, later Birmingham

New Street, on peak Saturdays and Bank Holidays from 4 August 1979, and occasional BR diesel locomotive-hauled long distance excursions.

The British Sugar Corporation sidings at Foley Park ceased to be used after early 1982, and in 1983-84 more than £370,000 was raised by share issue, £80,000 of which was employed to fund the purchase of the 1½ miles of railway between Foley Park and Kidderminster Junction. The balance of the share issue capital was used to develop the former BR goods yard site at Comberton Hill, Kidderminster, to form a new SVR passenger station, designated 'Kidderminster Town'. The 3½-mile section from Bewdley to Kidderminster Town was opened to passenger services on Monday 30 July 1984, and thus creating the last rail link in the present-day 16-mile-long Severn Valley Railway.

The first train to leave Kidderminster in preservation days starts its journey to Bridgnorth on Monday 30 July 1984 behind GWR 'Hall' Class 4-6-0 No 4930 *Hagley Hall*. *Brian Tromans*

THE TRAIN JOURNEY STATION-BY-STATION

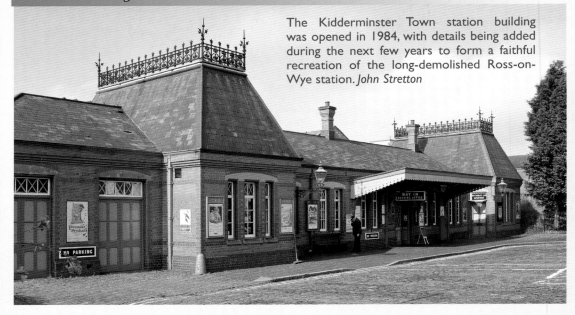

The Kidderminster Town station building was opened in 1984, with details being added during the next few years to form a faithful recreation of the long-demolished Ross-on-Wye station. *John Stretton*

The 16-mile journey over the Severn Valley line from Kidderminster to Bridgnorth provides visitors with some extremely fine views of the Severn valley that are denied to road visitors. The distances shown within brackets in the following text are measured from Kidderminster Town.

KIDDERMINSTER TOWN

Our journey starts at the SVR's own Kidderminster Town station, situated some 600 yards from the town centre, and less than 100 yards from the Network Rail passenger station. It was newly built in red brick to a traditional Great Western Railway turn-of-the-century design (Ross-on-Wye was the 'model') and opened in several stages from 1984 until the concourse glazed roof was completed in 2006. Facilities within the building include a sales shop, buffet and public house (the 'King and Castle'). As with most SVR stations today, the paintwork features the GWR colours of 'light and dark stone'.

The roomy booking hall where train tickets are purchased. It is decorated with information panels, maps, timetables, pictures and historic posters. *SVR Archive*

Station notes

Opened: 30 July 1984
Ownership: Severn Valley Railway
Platforms: two for passengers
Signal box: one
Toilets: yes
Café: yes
Shop: yes
Pub: yes
Access for the disabled: yes

The paved concourse area is protected by a glazed roof, constructed in 2006, that is a lighter-weight version of an original GWR design. It affords covered access to the platforms, the sales shop, bookstall, and, visible in this Santa season 2016 view, the 'King and Castle' public house on the left and the Refreshment Room on the right. *Bill Griffiths*

For your needs: the sales shop at Kidderminster Town sells a wide range of books and gifts, and model railway items too! The entrance is to the left of the one-time W. H. Smith bookstall, which was relocated here from Manchester Victoria station in 1989, and underneath the sign 'Station Emporium' (an old railway term). *David Mark*

KIDDERMINSTER TOWN STATION (Severn Valley)

Kidderminster Railway Museum

To Birmingham

Comberton Hill

Kidderminster Station (Network Rail)

carriage workshop

signal box

The Long Footbridge

turntable

diesel workshop

To Bridgnorth

To Worcester

Two views looking northwards to the bufferstops at Kidderminster Town station:
Above: Kidderminster Railway Museum, the former grain and wool warehouse, forms an impressive background to this scene from Platform 2, where the 'Warship' diesel-hydraulic B-B locomotive No D821 *Greyhound* is standing at the bufferstops ready to 'run round' its train on 19 September 2008. *Brian Harris*

Below: Swinging to the right from the view above, LMSR Stanier Class 5 2-6-0 No 42968 is in the course of running round its train in Platform 1 on 30 March 2008. A GWR Collett coach 4786 occupied the adjacent siding at the time. The twin-gabled roof denotes the concourse area of the station and the entrance to the platforms is gained to the left of the locomotive. *Peter Treloar*

A general view of the 'throat' of Kidderminster Town station. Visiting GWR 2-8-0 tank No 4270 is just departing from Platform 1 with a Bridgnorth train on 22 March 2015, during a busy Steam Gala event. Behind the loco is the 62-lever signalbox, built to a historic Great Western design, and completed in 1988. *Roger Norfolk*

Kidderminster Town station is on the site of Comberton Hill railway goods yard, which closed in 1982. The track layout is now entirely different from those days, with a central passenger platform that can accommodate a ten-coach train at each of the two platform faces, each with a run-round loop for locomotive release purposes.

KIDDERMINSTER TO BEWDLEY

Looking forward in the direction that our train leaves the station, first on the right is Kidderminster Railway Museum, a Trust organisation not owned by the SVR Company. Housed in the former railway grain and wool warehouse is a nationally recognised collection of historic railway exhibits. Next is the SVR car park, created on the site of the former coal yard, livestock pens and garage for railway-owned road motor vehicles. On the left, across the Network Rail car park, is the SVR carriage repair works, previously the railway goods shed that handled general merchandise traffic, in particular carpets, for the Kidderminster district.

Just beyond the platform end is the SVR's signal box, completed in 1988 to a standard Great Western Railway design of the steam age, and one of the largest installations in preservation. Next is the long footbridge across all the tracks, still known locally by the name of its predecessor, the 'wooden bridge'. A bridge here has been a feature of the local scene since it replaced a level crossing in the 19th century. The Network Rail Birmingham-Stourbridge-Worcester line on the left is now parallel to the Severn Valley line; its 1953-built Kidderminster Junction signal box, previously stood here until demolished in 2015.

Above: The original Kidderminster Goods Shed that handled general merchandise for over a century was converted to a Carriage Works when the site was bought for preservation. It carries out all major running gear maintenance and some bodywork and paintwork repairs to SVR-based carriages, although other carriage activity occurs at Bewdley and Bridgnorth. Here, the body of GWR–design inspection saloon No 80969 has been lifted by jacks, and the bogies rolled out for attention on 16 January 2015. *David Dawson*

Below: The 70-foot turntable from Fort William was relocated here at Kidderminster in 1994 and can turn the largest British steam locos, the LMSR and LNER Pacifics. This night scene shows GWR 4-6-0 No 7802 *Bradley Manor* enjoying a spin on 23 September 1995. *Jason Houlders*

Above: A maintenance depot for the SVR's fleet of diesel locomotives and railcars was constructed at Kidderminster and completed in 2016. In the view above, English Electric 2,700 hp Co-Co diesel-electric locos Nos 50 049/35/31 are lined up outside. *Jon Dunster*

Right: In the interior view, a wide variety of diesel locomotives is receiving attention in 2018. *Duncan Sealey*

Below: Kidderminster carriage shed, capable of housing 56 full-length passenger coaches, was opened in 2000. It protects the SVR fleet from the extremes of weather. In this scene, newly refurbished LMSR corridor third coach No 12992 is on view. *David Dawson*

At Kidderminster Junction until 1970, Severn Valley line passenger trains branched away from the Birmingham to Worcester 'main line' onto the route that we are now to follow. A rail connection between the SVR and Network Rail still exists here, and was renewed and upgraded in 2012.

On the right is the site of an extensive marshalling yard, active until 1984. Today, the north end of the site is occupied by a 70 foot long turntable that was formerly located at Fort William in the Scottish West Highlands from new in 1948 until 1967; it was relocated here in 1994. Next is the impressive diesel maintenance depot for the SVR's fleet of historic diesel locomotives, shunters and railcars. And at the south end of the site is the large four-track carriage shed, completed in 2000 thanks to a Heritage Lottery Fund grant. The necessarily functional structure can house up to 56 full-length coaches from the

Railway's operational fleet, protecting them from the ravages of the weather, and at one-fifth of a mile long, it is by far the largest building of its kind in preservation.

The line curves away to the right beyond the end of this building and into a low cutting spanned by Hoo Road bridge. From the left of this bridge, a trackside footpath formerly led to the second Kidderminster locomotive shed, active from 1932 until 1964. The shed site is now occupied by the housing estate seen on the left of the line. (The first Kidderminster locomotive shed, a small structure, was situated on the opposite side of the Network Rail line to Kidderminster goods shed from 1852 until 1932.)

The railway leaves this confined area and enters a long straight section, carried on a high embankment pierced by a bridge over the A449 Kidderminster to Worcester road, then by the seven-arch 132-yard-long Falling Sands Viaduct,

Visiting British Railways Standard Class 9F 2-10-0 No 92214 crosses Falling Sands viaduct, Kidderminster, with a train to Bridgnorth on 21 March 2017. The viaduct is 132 feet long and 64 feet high, and its 7 arches span the River Stour and the Staffordshire and Worcestershire Canal in quick succession. The canal boat *Windrush* shares the stage in this sunny scene. *Alan Corfield*

Above: The 478 yard long Bewdley tunnel pierces the sandstone ridge that separates the Stour valley at Foley Park with the Severn valley at Bewdley. Here the Royal Train, conveying TRH The Prince of Wales and The Duchess of Cornwall on a visit to the SVR, leaves the tunnel in the charge of visiting GWR 4-6-0 No 6024 *King Edward I* on 10 June 2008, a glorious summer day. *Chris Wright*

Below: Arguably the most famous steam locomotive in the world, the LNER Gresley A3 Class 4-6-2 No 60103 *Flying Scotsman,* climbs the 1 in 100 gradient from Bewdley to the tunnel with a Bridgnorth to Kidderminster train on 25 September 2016.   After a major repair programme, this National Railway Museum York-based engine was spending a sell-out week on the SVR pulling the Railway's set of nine LNER Gresley varnished teak carriages, filled to capacity with passengers each day. *Bob Green*

crossing successively the River Stour and James Brindley's Staffordshire & Worcestershire Canal of 1770. Here, on clear days, the distinctive Malvern Hills may be glimpsed on the horizon 20 miles away to the left, while to the right is a view of central Kidderminster. The track continues to rise on a 1 in 115 gradient, passing on the left the site of the British Sugar Corporation beet factory, the extensive sidings and rail system of which were active until 1982. This area is being redeveloped. The site of **Foley Park Halt** was on the right adjacent to the road overbridge.

The line then reaches an easily discernable summit in the deepening cutting shortly before plunging into the 478-yard Bewdley tunnel, located on a long descent, mostly at 1 in 100. This tunnel, often referred to, perhaps more appropriately, as Foley Park tunnel, is mostly straight, with a slight curve at the Bewdley end. By this means, the line emerges dramatically from the Birchen Coppice escarpment into the open country of the Severn Valley. There is agricultural land and Bewdley's grass-strip airport to the left and the heathland of the 'Rifle Range' and the tree-topped sandstone outcrop of The Devil's Spittleful to the right. **Rifle Range Halt** was once situated nearby.

Continuing the descent, alongside on the right is the southern boundary of the Spring Grove Estate. This has been occupied since 1973 by the West Midland Safari Park, and glimpses of world wildlife, including elephants and hippos, may be obtained from the right-hand side of the train. The line then enters the deep cutting that precedes the junction, on the left, with the route of the original Severn Valley line of 1862 from Hartlebury and Stourport to Bewdley South Junction, which was severed in 1973. The first half-mile of the trackbed, to Mount Pleasant tunnel, was bought by the SVR in 1982, and the track was relaid for filming purposes, then later cut back as an engineer's siding.

We have now completed the journey over the whole length of the Great Western Railway's Kidderminster to Bewdley 'loop line' of 1878, and the train is now travelling on the route of the Severn Valley Railway proper. The crossing of the 1987-built bridge over the A456 Bewdley bypass is immediately followed by the 101-yard Sandbourne Viaduct of ten arches, high above a pool on the Spring Grove Estate.

One of the elephants in the West Midland Safari Park's herd appears to be taking an interest in GWR small Prairie tank No 4566 as it strides out of Bewdley with a Bridgnorth to Kidderminster train on 1 October 2011. *Scott Lewis*

Above: This is the one-time Bewdley South Junction, where the original Severn Valley line of 1862 (on the left) was joined from 1878 onwards by the so-named 'Kidderminster loop' (on the right). The original line from here to Stourport and Hartlebury is now merely a short siding, but the Kidderminster line is part of the present Severn Valley Railway route; this is demonstrated by Britain's newest mainline steam locomotive, the LNER A1 4-6-2 No 60163 *Tornado*, accelerating its train over Sandbourne viaduct and Bewdley by-pass bridge on 31 October 2009. *Alan Corfield*

Below: This impressive array of semaphore signals denotes the approach to Bewdley. Port Talbot Railway 0-6-0 saddle tank No 26, restored as GWR No 813, climbs sturdily past Bewdley South signalbox with a train to Kidderminster on 4 November 2016. *Neville Wellings*

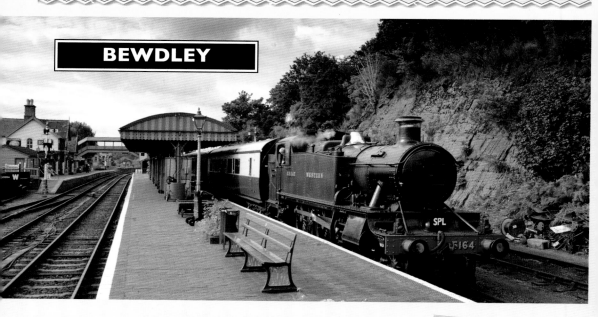

BEWDLEY

A timeless scene at Bewdley, featuring a typical Great Western train of the 1930s and 1940s. Large Prairie tank No 5164 and matching coaches stand at Platform 3 with a charter passenger train on 18 September 2013. *Lewis Maddox*

The 1877-built Bewdley South signal box on the right is situated in a short sandstone cutting that forms the entrance to the one-time double junction station of Bewdley (3½ miles). This was the southerly passenger terminus of the Severn Valley Railway service from Bridgnorth between 1974 and 1984. To the left, the main Bewdley station building, of red-brick construction, is fronted by a single platform that can accommodate five coaches. On the right is the island platform capable of holding eight-coach trains at each platform face and equipped with a long awning roof. This historic infrastructure provides the opportunity to display such early period features as signs, advertisements, posters, milk churns, cabin trunks, etc, and, of course, hanging flower baskets in season. A more permanent feature on the island platform is the cast-iron gents urinal brought from Melrose station in the Scottish borders.

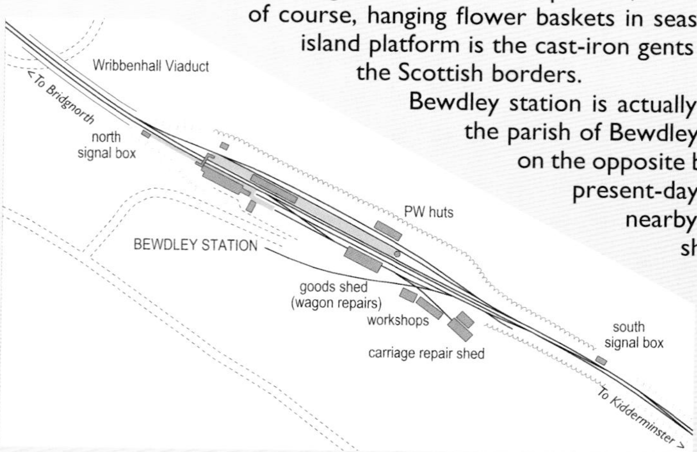

Bewdley station is actually situated in the parish of Wribbenhall; the parish of Bewdley, and indeed the town itself, is situated on the opposite bank of the River Severn to the left. The present-day SVR occupies the main station building; nearby there is a buffet coach and railwayane shop and in the sidings to the south of the station repairs are carried out to rolling stock. All of the wagons on the line are repaired in and around the former goods shed, which in an earlier age was busy dealing with the merchandise and produce of the local area.

Station notes

Opened: 1 February 1862
Ownership: Severn Valley Railway (twice!)
Platforms: three
Signal boxes: two
Toilets: yes
Café: yes (coach)
Shop: railwayana
Pub: no
Disabled access: platform 1, yes; platforms 2 and 3, staff assistance needed over boarded crossing

Diagram labels:
< To Bridgnorth
Wribbenhall Viaduct
north signal box
BEWDLEY STATION
PW huts
goods shed (wagon repairs)
workshops
carriage repair shed
south signal box
To Kidderminster >

Above: GWR 0-6-0 pannier tank No 5764 makes a spirited start from Platform 2 at Bewdley for Kidderminster on 19 September 2008. This is another authentic railway scene recalling the Bewdley of eighty years ago. *Chris Wright*

Left: Bewdley south signal box. *Pat Arrowsmith*

Below: Visiting GWR 4-6-0 No 7820 *Dinmore Manor* stands in Platform 1 at Bewdley station during an evening photographic event for enthusiasts on 12 November 2016. *Malcolm Ranieri*

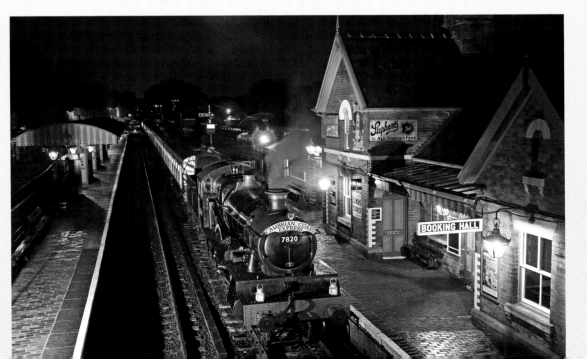

Visiting SR Bulleid-designed 'Battle of Britain' 4-6-2 No 34081 *92 Squadron* arrives at Bewdley by means of the ten-arch 128-yard-long Wribbenhall viaduct with a charter train on 20 March 2017. *John Titlow*

BEWDLEY TO ARLEY

As the train leaves Bewdley, the line begins to keep company with the River Severn on the left; indeed, it is never more than half a mile away from the river for the remainder of the journey to Bridgnorth. Immediately, Bewdley North signal box of 1877 is passed on the left, before we cross the 112-yard-long Bewdley (Wribbenhall) Viaduct of eight arches, which spans the former main Kidderminster to Ludlow road. From this viaduct, and the following embankment, passengers have a commanding view to the left of Bewdley's Georgian roof-tops and waterfront, and Thomas Telford's 1798 bridge across the Severn leading to St Anne's church in the centre of the main thoroughfare of Load Street.

The apparent double-track formation of the line was always operated from Bewdley as two single lines, reducing to a single track as the course of the Wyre Forest line to Tenbury Wells (closed completely in 1965) dropped away to the left, the two routes initially being separated by a stone retaining wall. The Tenbury line curved

Closed connections

Today there is a choice of two destinations by train from Bewdley – Bridgnorth and Kidderminster. But before 1962 the choice was four, with the addition of Hartlebury (to change for Worcester) and Wooferton via Tenbury Wells (to change for Ludlow and Leominster). So you can see that, before the widespread advent of road motor transport, Bewdley station was an important (and bustling) transport interchange for passengers and goods over a wide area of the West Midlands.

The Tenbury line opened to passengers one year after the Severn Valley line, and closed to through traffic one year before it – thus 99 years for the Tenbury line, and 101 years for the Severn Valley.

to cross above Northwood Lane, then spanned the River Severn by means of Dowles Bridge, the stone piers of which defied economical demolition and remain largely intact. The Tenbury line then disappeared into the depths of the Wyre Forest, whilst our line passes close to the distinctive stone dwelling of Northwood Cottage.

With the line clinging to the valley side, the formal Bewdley caravan sites give way to the more informal holiday chalets so characteristic of this area. Also, the green pastures of the valley floor give way to the woodland of North Wood as we approach, on the right, the request stop of

NORTHWOOD HALT

The unstaffed halt here opened on Monday 17 June 1935, and originally featured a simple wooden waiting shelter on a short ash-covered timber edged platform. It was popular with fishermen, and lasted until the cessation of BR services in 1963. The halt was reopened on 18 May 1974, soon to receive a large slatted timber hut; this was replaced in 2006 by a newly constructed GWR corrugated-iron 'pagoda roofed' shelter. Today Northwood is a request stop, although it is not included in the public timetable, except by reference note.

Northwood Halt (5 miles), immediately preceded by a level-crossing carrying a minor private road. This crossing is now protected by light signals and an audible warning, replacing the hand-operated gates of earlier times.

Shortly after Northwood, the impressive bridge that carries the Elan Aqueduct over the River Severn appears on the left, before the connecting pipeline passes beneath the railway. The 73-mile-long aqueduct has been the main water supply pipeline to the City of Birmingham since 1904, and gravity feeds from a series of reservoirs in the Elan Valley in Powys, central Wales, to Frankley Reservoir in Birmingham.

Severe reverse curves denote the passage of Folly Point, which is the narrowest part of the valley in this vicinity, with the river 40 feet below track level on the left, flanked by wooded slopes. The line climbs past the attractively situated Trimpley Reservoirs, the largest of which is host to sailing dinghies that add colour to the scene at holiday periods. The river here is out of sight beyond and below the reservoirs. The line then descends through Eymore Wood cutting to emerge onto Victoria Bridge over the River Severn.

Victoria Bridge is the most photographed location on the line, and is at its best when autumnal colours break out in Eymore Wood to the right. It has been well used by film and TV companies. The bridge, incorporating – at 200 feet – the longest cast-iron clear span in the world when built, was designed by the first SVR's Engineer-in-Chief, Sir John Fowler, and completed in 1861. This work was finished some 30 years before his participation in the design and construction of the massive and iconic Forth Railway Bridge in Scotland. From here onwards the railway keeps the river on its right-hand side, and climbs up on a high embankment and through a deep cutting ('The Great Cutting') to Arley station.

There are few more iconic Great Western branch line scenes than a pagoda-style waiting room and an Auto (push-and-pull) train. Here Collett 0-4-2 tank No 1450 stands at Northwood Halt, a request stop 1½ miles north of Bewdley, on 18 April 2013. *Charles Adams*

Eymore Wood views:

Above: A southbound train from Bridgnorth to Kidderminster skirts the higher (most northerly) of the two Trimpley reservoirs shortly after leaving Arley. The expanse of the woodland forms an impressive backdrop. The train of BR standard Mark 1 coaches in carmine-and-cream livery is headed by LMR Ivatt Class 4 2-6-0 No 43106 on 3 December 2011. *Andrew Bell*

Below: The superb prospect of the 1861-built Victoria Bridge spanning the River Severn is seen here from a point near the road linking Button Oak in the Wyre Forest with Arley. An all-LMSR train, consisting of visiting 'Crab' 2-6-0 No 13065 (BR No 42765) pulling the SVR's train of Stanier coaches, negotiates the bridge at the foot of the short climb to Arley station. This is a Kidderminster to Bridgnorth journey on 4 November 2016. *Alan Corfield*

SOUTH OF ARLEY:

Above: With the hillside of Seckley Wood on the horizon, LMR Ivatt Class 2 2-6-0 No 46443 climbs from Victoria Bridge towards Arley station at the head of a Kidderminster to Bridgnorth train on 26 Novenber 2010. *Mick Flint*

Below: Turning through 180°, this is the view of 'The Great Cutting' on a snowy 19 December 2010, as LMSR Stanier Class 5 2-6-0 No 42968 sets out from Arley station with a Santa Special returning to Kidderminster. *Bob Green*

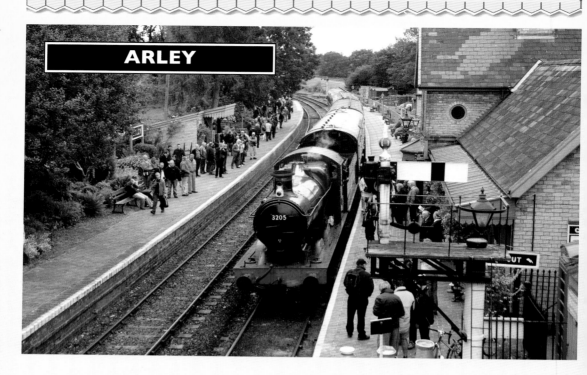

Arley station is viewed from the road bridge at the south end of the platforms. GWR Collett 2251 class 0-6-0 No 3205 calls with a southbound train during the Autumn steam gala on 26 September 2010. *David A Smith*

Arley station (7 miles), is at the north end of 'The Great Cutting', which is spanned by the minor road from the hamlet of Button Oak, in the Wyre Forest, to the Arley riverside. This road leads 300 yards away to the right, past 'The Harbour' public house (the last remaining of six in the village!), and terminates at the disused western ferry ramp by the footbridge across the River Severn. The footbridge, built in 1973 to replace a passenger river current operated ferry, links directly to the village of Upper Arley on the opposite bank.

Across the footbridge, to the left a road leads past the general store and café, then above the eastern ferry ramp and up the hill past the former 'Valentia Arms'. It terminates by the gated entrance to Arley Arboretum; these are the grounds of Arley House, although unfortunately the house itself, sometimes referred to as Arley Castle, was demolished in 1960. A private road continues to the left of the gated entrance up to the picturesque 12th-century red sandstone church of St Peter. The churchyard here has a magnificent view of the valley and its trains. Turning right after crossing the footbridge leads to a riverside walk under Victoria Bridge to Trimpley Reservoirs.

Arley station is a most attractive one, and located in a beautiful setting. Immediately to the right, the main Arley station building, of yellow brick in typical Severn Valley Railway style, is complemented by a small neat waiting shelter on the opposite platform. The lower slope of the hill on the left has been landscaped, and there is added floral colour in season. A refreshment kiosk has been built at the entrance to the station, and there is also a gift shop further along the drive. A seated picnic area is available near the kiosk.

There had been a passing loop and two platforms at Arley since line improvements in 1883, but the loop and the northbound platform were removed by BR in 1964, and had to be reinstated by SVR volunteers in 1974. (The correct platform blue bricks were brought from the long-closed station at Stoke Works, near Bromsgrove!) The original signal box was demolished in 1967, and replaced in 1976 by the then recently closed LNWR signal box from Yorton, near Whitchurch, Shropshire. Today, this controls not only the loop but also two reinstated sidings.

Left: A view at the north end of Arley station. GWR 4-6-0 No 7812 *Erlestoke Manor* calls with a fund-raising special train bound for Bridgnorth on 1 June 2011. *Bob Sweet*

Station notes

Opened: 1 February 1862
Ownership: Severn Valley Railway
Platforms: two
Signal box: one
Toilets: yes
Café: kiosk
Shop: yes (gifts)
Pub: no
Disabled access: platform 1, yes; platform 2 via boarded crossing

...ow: An early preservation scene, ...LMSR 'Jinty' 3F 0-6-0 tank ...47383, pulling a demonstration ...ods train, passes Summer Gala ...tors at Arley on 24 June 1984. ...vid C.Williams

< To Bridgnorth

signal box

ARLEY STATION

To Kidderminster >

What's in a name?

Bewdley station is in Wribbenhall, Highley station is in Stanley, and Hampton Loade station is in Hampton! Although Arley station is in Woodeaves, habitation here is very sparse, and the station principally serves the village of Upper Arley, on the opposite bank of the river.

ARLEY TO HIGHLEY

The journey north of Arley continues through picturesque riverside scenery in a particularly quiet and unspoilt part of the valley. The woodland on the left near Bank Farm effectively forms the eastern boundary of the Wyre Forest, an area of outstanding natural beauty. After nearly a mile, at Severn Lodge, we pass from Worcestershire into Shropshire, although the opposite river bank remains within Worcestershire for a further mile.

On a straight section of line, the wider trackbed of Kinlet sidings is just discernable on the left of the line. Today it is difficult to believe that Kinlet was a busy railway location from 1880 onwards, with an impressive signal box, extant from 1913 until 1943. It controlled the interchange sidings with a private branch line to the collieries at Billingsley (closed 1921) and Kinlet (closed 1935), which curved sharply off to the left up the valley of the Borle Brook. This tributary of the Severn is immediately crossed by means of the 42-yard four-arch Borle Viaduct, near its confluence with the big river. Immediately the line passes over a private road to the riverside at Coomby's (or Fishermen's) Crossing. Visible to the right are the restored mine manager's and clerk's houses near the cast-iron Brooksmouth bridge of 1828. A little further on, the line curves to the left through the deep sandstone walls of Stanley cutting, followed by a right-hand curve that signals the approach to Highley.

Right: Arguably the second most famous British steam locomotive is LMSR 4-6-0 No 6100 *Royal Scot* of 1927. Here, as BR No 46100, the locomotive is approaching Borle viaduct, heading a Bridgnorth to Kidderminster train on 20 September 2015. *Phil Jones*

Below: The four arches of the viaduct over the Borle Brook, a tributary of the River Severn, are easily visible in this winter view taken on 10 November 2010. Ivatt Class 4 2-6-0 No 43106 is heading a Bridgnorth to Kidderminster train one mile south of Highley. *Mick Flint*

As the train approaches Highley station, The Engine House, our Visitor & Education Centre, comes into view.

This dramatic building is on the site of Alveley Colliery's 'Landsale Yard', a long narrow flat area of hard-standing which was adjacent to the foot of a steep rope-worked incline to Highley Colliery, active from 1874 until 1940. This site had become an overgrown wilderness, and in 2001 was purchased by two SVR members with future railway use in mind.

Major funding for the visitor centre was provided by the Heritage Lottery Fund, the European Regional Development Fund, Advantage West Midlands and Bridgnorth District Council, with additional help from SVR members and shareholders.

Work started on The Engine House in 2005, and it opened to the public on Good Friday, 21 March 2008. It sees over 60,000 visitors per year and usually houses approximately eight out-of-service locomotives from the reserve fleet. Other coaches and wagons complete this exciting exhibition, the foremost being King George VI's royal carriage and a travelling post office coach. Access to some of the exhibits depends on the availability of guides.

These full-size exhibits are surrounded by displays, relics and models of railway and local interest, together with audio visual presentations and other special effects.

On the first floor, the restaurant is an ideal place for a light bite or a full meal and is flanked on one side by an internal balcony with a view of the locomotives in the main exhibition hall, and on the other side by an external balcony giving a pleasing panorama of the Severn valley, the line and its trains.

The main hall of The Engine House at Highley is seen on 13 September 2016, revealing part of the collection of steam locomotives assembled within. *Lewis Maddox*

Back on the ground floor, there is a gift shop, plus an outside picnic area with seating and tables, together with a children's adventure playground.

The Engine House is an easy 150 yard walk from Highley station and is fully disability compliant, including the provision of a lift to the first floor.

The view from the balcony of The Engine House, where visitors can enjoy a meal or a snack whilst viewing passing trains with the River Severn as a backdrop. LMSR Stanier Class 5 2-6-0 No 42968 excites interest on 31 August 2009. *Lewis Maddox*

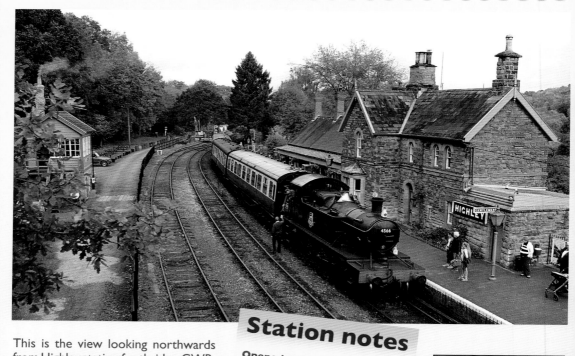

This is the view looking northwards from Highley station footbridge; GWR small Prairie tank No 4566, running here in early BR black livery, is calling with a train to Kidderminster on 26 October 2016. *John Oates*

Station notes

Opened: 1 February 1862
Ownership: Severn Valley Railway
Platform: one
Signal box: one
Toilets: yes
Café: kiosk
Shop: yes (books & magazines(
Pub: no
Disabled access: over boarded crossing, staff assistance required

The railway enters Highley across a bridge spanning the minor road from Highley village to the riverside, terminating at 'The Ship Inn'. The direct foot access to the inn is through a gate from the station platform and down a steep path towards the river. Highley station (9½ miles) is located on a sharp right-hand curve with a single platform on the right, a passing loop, siding and signal box on the left, and a restored cattle dock also on the left. Trains can pass here, but operationally, only one of them can be a passenger train. A mellow stone station building, comprising the ticket office, waiting room, staff room and toilets, stands on the platform, directly opposite the signal box. There is also a refreshment kiosk and shop sellinh books and magazines.

Although very little had changed at Highley since BR days, the buildings and surroundings were in a poor and dirty state on the eve of preservation. A remarkable transformation has taken place, which considerably enhanced the appearance of the area to the visitor. A footbridge at the south end of the platform was in use from 1915 until 1973, when it was declared dangerous, demolished and replaced by a boarded crossing. However, as part of a safe walking route to 'The Engine House', a brand new footbridge was erected, and opened on 21 October 2009.

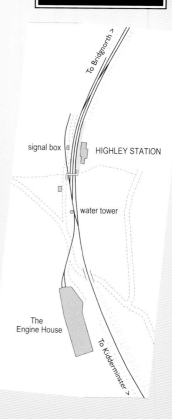

HIGHLEY

To Bridgnorth
signal box
HIGHLEY STATION
water tower
The Engine House
To Kidderminster

Above: Visitors to The Engine House have a fine view from the terrace of LNER A4 4-6-2 No 4464 (BR No 60019) *Bittern* approaching Highley station during the Spring Steam Gala on 23 March 2012. This scene was recorded from the balcony. *Neville Wellings*

Below: A view from Highley footbridge looking southwards, with The Engine House visible in the background. WR 15xx 0-6-0 pannier tank No 1501 is performing a shunting movement during the Spring Steam Gala on 17 April 2016. *Peter Marsh*

HIGHLEY TO HAMPTON LOADE

Leaving Highley, there follows a severe test for the locomotives of northbound trains, with a 1 in 60 gradient on a sharp right-hand curve away from the end of the platform. The summit of the climb is reached on an equally severe left-hand curve shortly before the location of a foot crossing of the line. This was used from 1939 until 1969 by miners walking from homes in Highley village (away to the left) to Alveley Colliery (on the right), accessed by a concrete bridge across the river, built in 1937. The bridge now provides pedestrian access to the Severn Valley Country Park, on the site of one of Alveley Colliery's spoil tips. The aforementioned foot crossing precedes the site of Alveley Halt, known locally as Alveley Miners' Halt, on the left.

A little to the north of Alveley Halt, to the right on a straight and level section of the line, there was once a busy railway marshalling yard containing four sidings where coal from the colliery was loaded, and beyond which was the coal washing plant and ancillary equipment. After the 1969 colliery closure, all of this infrastructure gradually disappeared from the landscape, to be replaced in more recent times by picnic seats and tables! This is also the location of the unstaffed Country Park Halt (10½ miles).

Beyond the Alveley colliery site, the line passes milepost 144½ (from London Paddington

COUNTRY PARK HALT (UNSTAFFED)

Opened on Thursday 4 April 1996, the unstaffed red-brick Country Park Halt (10½ miles) cost £75,000 and was funded by Bridgnorth District Council, Shropshire County Council and the European Regional Development Fund. The Halt serves the nearby Severn Valley Country Park across the river.

A view of the Country Park Halt request stop looking northwards. GWR 4-6-0 No 7802 *Bradley Manor* is emerging from the woodland section from Hampton Loade and is passing the Halt with a Bridgnorth to Kidderminster train on 12 September 2017. *John Oates*

via Worcester), which was the boundary between BR and the SVR from 1970 until 1974. This marks the commencement of a woodland section that extends on both sides of the line for more than half a mile. Alongside, for most of the way, the line is flanked on the right by National Cycle Route 45, from Chester to Gloucester and Salisbury. This part of the route – 'The Mercian Way' – was developed and promoted by Shropshire County Council with close SVR co-operation, and opened on Thursday 4 April 1996. Approaching Hampton Loade, the forest disappears, and to the right is a superb elevated view of the river at close quarters.

Above: Just south of Hampton Loade, the Railway route offers a fine view of the River Severn below, as seen here. GWR large Prairie tank No 5164 is making a spirited exit from the station with a Bridgnorth to Kidderminster train on 12 April 2009. 'The Mercian Way' cycle path is visible in front of the loco.
Paul Pearson

Below: A general view of Hampton Loade station looking northwards, with visiting GWR large Prairie tank No 4160 appearing from Bridgnorth light engine on 23 September 2011. *David Wllcock*

The classic view of Hampton Loade station is shown here. LM Ivatt Class 2 2-6-2 tank No 41312 is heading a charter train for photographers on 21 June 2017. Locomotives of this type were used on the Severn Valley line in its final 12 months of BR operation in 1962-3. *Alan Corfield*

HAMPTON LOADE

Hampton Loade station (11½ miles) is an archetypal country station. In GWR and BR days it was a popular destination for fishermen and day-trippers, being a tranquil spot very near to the landing ramp for a passenger chain ferry across the river. The station is attractively situated, and was the first to be extensively restored by members of the SVR Society between 1967 and 1970. The main station building, of yellow brick, is on the left, opposite a yellow brick waiting room with timber extension on the right. Here there is a refreshment kiosk, and nearby a railway book and railwayana shop. The passing loop dates from line improvements in 1883, when the second platform and a siding, both on the right, were added. The station assumed great importance as the southern terminus of the passenger service at the start of the preservation era from 1970 to 1974.

Station notes

Opened: 1 February 1862
Ownership: Severn Valley Railway
Platforms: two
Signal box: one
Toilets: yes
Café: kiosk
Shop: yes books and railwayane
Pub: no
Disabled access: yes

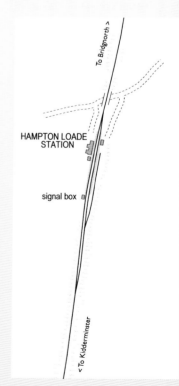

To Bridgnorth >

HAMPTON LOADE
STATION

signal box

< To Kidderminster

Above: The waiting shelter on Platform 2 at Hampton Loade station oversees the impressive arrival of SR 'West Country' 4-6-2 No 34027 *Taw Valley* from Bridgnorth on 12 August 2015. *Malcolm Ranieri*

Below: A northbound train arrives at Platform 1 at Hampton Loade station headed by 'Western' class diesel-hydraulic C-C No D1062 *Western Courier* on 7 July 2016. *David Bissett*

HAMPTON LOADE TO EARDINGTON

Immediately after Hampton Loade station the line passes over the minor road from Chelmarsh to the Hampton riverside at the former ferry landing ramp. A short cutting precedes a boarded crossing on the footpath leading to 'The Unicorn' public house, which is immediately to the right of the railway. The line then passes above riverside fields to the right, the first of which is occupied by tents and holiday caravans in season. Half a mile north, a private road linking Chelmarsh (left) crosses the railway at the gated Waterworks Crossing, and spans the river by means of a bridge shared with, and supported by, twin curved water pipelines.

We are now entering a picturesque part of the valley, with the woodland area of Long Covert visible on the opposite riverbank, covering a hillside through which a footpath leads to Dudmaston Hall (out of sight). Speed will be reduced in Little Rock cutting at the start of the left-hand curve below New House Farm, which is situated high above the line on the left-hand side. Sterns is the location of a vunerable section of track that receives constant inspection. Sterns Cottage, on the right, is near the coppice of that name on the left, with the Mor Brook tributary passing beneath the line immediately afterwards. This is at the foot of the 1½-mile climb to Eardington summit, mostly at a gradient of 1 in 100. The line crosses the B4555 Highley to Bridgnorth road at Hay (or Haye) Bridge, and enters a steep-sided sandstone cutting, spanned at the north end by an occupation bridge on the approach to Eardington station.

Between Hampton Loade and Eardington, the views of the River Severn from the train are particularly fine. This is evident in this view of LMSR 'Jubilee' 4-6-0 No 5690 (BR No 45690) *Leander*, heading a Bridgnorth to Kidderminster train recovering from the permanent way restriction at Sterns on 25 September 2010. Above the loco at this elevation can be glimpsed Dudmaston Hall. *Alan Corfield*

SR Maunsell U Class 2-6-0 No 31806 performs a run-past at Eardington station for photographers who chartered this train on 16 October 2014. The siding on the right is used for loading and unloading permanent way materials. *Andrew Bell*

EARDINGTON (CLOSED)

Nowadays closed to passengers, Eardington station is situated in a remote location amidst mixed farming country near the sites of two historic iron-making forges, Upper Forge near the halt, and Lower Forge by the river. Eardington opened as a station on Monday 1 June 1868, five years after the opening of the whole line, and was reduced to unstaffed status (although never deemed a 'Halt') after 1 April 1949. The goods loop here was reduced to a siding, accessed from the south, after 1959, and lifted in 1964.

Eardington station is better known for its 'second life' (when it was deemed a 'Halt'), even though it is closed to passengers again nowadays. When the SVR reopened from Bridgnorth to Hampton Loade (only) on 23 May 1970, Eardington could be justified as the only intermediate stop. There was the added bonus of a ready supply of good-quality water here, and a locomotive water tank from Withymoor goods yard, near Dudley, was rapidly installed. The original brick station building on the solid platform was restored, and other restoration work done, but passenger interest was weak, as indeed was always the case, for the villages of Eardington and Chelmarsh are some distance away. Eardington Halt closed for repair work on Sunday 29 October 1978, then reopened as a request stop for specified trains on Saturday 7 March 1981, but this facility was withdrawn from Sunday 31 October 1982. The siding fared better, for it was relaid yet again as a loop in 1973, and reduced to a siding, accessed from the south, for permanent way operations in 1974. The Eardington site is still well maintained by a small group of volunteers, culminating in the collapsed south end of the platform being reinstated by them in 2018.

EARDINGTON TO BRIDGNORTH

After Eardington station, the line passes beneath the B4555 road at Eardington Bridge, and enters another steep-sided cutting, emerging alongside Daddy Wood on the right, into a natural amphitheatre much loved by railway photographers. The climb continues to Eardington summit, just beyond the Crossing Cottage of 1859 on the right, which is situated between two farm occupation overbridges. At the summit, 210 feet above sea level, the River Severn is now half a mile from the railway, and the line descends at 1 in 100 for 1½ miles, entering a deep cutting in the process. This is punctuated by the short 40-yard-long Knowlesands tunnel, passing under the B4555 road again, although it is not visible at this location. On the left is an industrial estate on the site of the quarry of Bridgnorth brickworks, once one of the largest in the area and served by two railway sidings from 1921 until 1948. The line then crosses the five-arch 87-yard-long Oldbury Viaduct above the restored Daniel's Mill, with its 38-foot-diameter wheel powered by water from two leats (supply pools). The mill produces flour for baking purposes. The viaduct was built to accommodate a double-track formation.

On the outskirts of Bridgnorth, the line emerges from Oldbury cutting onto an embankment and bridges the A458 southern bypass road just west of its viaduct across the River Severn on the right. The construction of the bypass occupied the years from 1982 until 1985. The high embankment continues, affording to the right a fine view across the river to Hermitage Hill and, nearer at hand, Castle Hill as we cross the B4363 Bridgnorth to Cleobury Mortimer road just outside Bridgnorth station.

Visiting GWR 'Modified Hall' 4-6-0 No 6990 *Witherslack Hall* bursts out of the short 40 yard long Knowlesands tunnel on the 1 in 100 climb to Eardington summit with a Bridgnorth to Kidderminster train on 24 March 2016. *Phil Jones*

Left: The five-arch Oldbury viaduct on the outskirts of Bridgnorth is crossed in restrained manner by visiting LMSR Stanier 8P 4-6-2 No 46233 *Duchess of Sutherland* and train of matching BR standard Mark 1 coaches bound for Kidderminster on 21 September 2013.
Alan Corfield

Below: At the other end of the passenger train spectrum, GWR Collett 1P 0-4-2 tank No 1450 crosses Oldbury viaduct on the snowy 26 March 2013 with push-and-pull auto coach *Chaffinch* in tow. The train forms a Hampton Loade to Bridgnorth shuttle service during the Spring Steam Gala. The visitor attraction of Daniel's Mill is in the foreground. *Phil Jones*

BRIDGNORTH

Bridgnorth station's Platform 1 welcomes the arrival of a train from Kidderminster in the charge of WR Hawksworth 0-6-0 pannier tank No 1501 in 2015. *SVR Archive*

Station notes

Opened: 1 February 1862
Ownership: Severn Valley Railway
Platforms: two
Signal box: one (formerly two)
Toilets: yes
Café: yes
Shop: yes
Pub: yes
Disabled access: platform 1, yes; platform 2, over boarded crossing, staff assistance required

In pre-preservation days Bridgnorth station (16 miles) served this important township on the 40¾-mile journey from Hartlebury to Shrewsbury, 18¼ miles from Hartlebury and 22½ miles from Shrewsbury. Today, however, it is the northern terminus of the line, and was the birthplace of the preservation scheme in 1965.

The listed main station building on Platform 1 on the right, built in 1861 in mellow stone, is faced on the opposite Platform 2 by a red-brick waiting shelter, added when the original 1862 track layout was expanded in 1887. Platform 1 can accommodate nine coaches, while Platform 2 takes six coaches. The slightly staggered platforms upon which the buildings are situated are linked by a footbridge, also new in 1887 and extensively refurbished in 2004.

From 1892 Bridgnorth boasted a signal box at each end of the station, but these were replaced by just one, on the present site, in 1922. That box was closed in 1963 and almost demolished by BR in 1965. A new signal box upper structure, from Pensnett, near Dudley, was installed by volunteers in 1969. Station facilities here include 'The Railwayman's Arms' on Platform 1, a fairly recent name for the public house in the station building, with a continuous record of opening from 1861 until the present day. Also on Platform 1 is a comprehensive

boiler shop

store

locomotive works

signal box

footbridge

BRIDGNORTH STATION

To Kidderminster >

Right: The entrance to Bridgnorth station – part of the original structure of 1861 – is viewed from the approach drive on 15 September 2016. *John Oates*

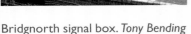

Bridgnorth signal box. *Tony Bending*

Centre: GWR Collett 0-6-0 pannier tank No 5764 is soon to leave Platform 2 of Bridgnorth with a special train to Kidderminster on 26 July 2008. *Brian Harris*

Below: This is an artist's impression of the new refreshment building at the south end of Platform 1 at Bridgnorth station, following a GWR design of *circa* 1900. Construction of this commenced in 2017 at the start of a wider redevelopment programme for the Bridgnorth site.

railway book and gift shop, the booking office, a refreshment room and toilet facilities.

Bridgnorth station site occupies a large area quite close to the centre of this historic medieval town, which comprises both a Low Town and a High Town. The entrance to the station is linked directly to New Road by means of a long footbridge. The first footbridge here was built by Rubery & Company in 1895 and closed in 1976; the present replacement was provided by donations to Bridgnorth Footbridge Trust, and opened in 1994.

On Castle Hill can be found the well-maintained gardens containing the sloping ruin of the 11th-century castle tower. From the gardens there are fine views over the River Severn, Low Town, and the site of the 11th-century fortification of Pan Pudding Hill, visible on the opposite side of the railway line. High Town and Low Town are linked directly over a steep 111-foot-high sandstone cliff by the famous Cliff Railway, completed in 1892 and still in daily operation today.

A general view looking northwards from Bridgnorth station footbridge of Platform 2 and the adjacent locomotive yard on 3 August 2017. The yard is occupied by GWR Collett 5700 0-6-0 pannier tank No 7714 and the impressive 30-ton steam crane. Beyond are the locomotive works buildings, comprising the mechanical workshop, the machine shop and the boiler shop. Out of sight on the far side is the paint shop. *John Oates*

Bridgnorth is the SVR's locomotive headquarters, and in the buildings to the left of the train all of the railway's steam locomotives are maintained, and heavy repairs are carried out. Machine shop work is performed inside the 1863-built stone building in the centre of the complex, which was formerly the railway goods shed, while mechanical repairs are carried out in the large 1977-built four-road shed to the south, and boiler repairs in the 1989-built distinctively roofed boiler shop to the north.

Did you know?

Most of the locomotives and coaches on the Severn Valley Railway have been in preservation service longer than they were in the ownership of the railways for which they were built. The newest steam locomotive in the fleet, 4MT 4-6-0 No 75069, was built by British Railways in 1955 and taken out of service in 1966, after only 11 years. After languishing in a scrapyard it was rescued, and has been on the Severn Valley Railway since 1974 – 38 years. The same does not apply, however, to our oldest loco, *The Lady Armaghdale*, which was built at Leeds in 1898!

Above: British Railways Standard Class 4 4-6-0 No 75069 is shown on 23 November 2017 during the course of major repairs in the mechanical workshop, the most prominent of the four main buildings that comprise Bridgnorth Locomotive Works. *John Oates*

Below: A very busy scene in Bridgnorth boiler works during March 2014, where the work of locomotive boiler-making and repairing is quite different from the mechanical work on steam locomotives. *Duncan Ballard*

The way north…a morning train from Bridgnorth to Shrewsbury crosses Hollybush Road and heads into Bridgnorth tunnel behind LM Ivatt Class 2 2-6-2 tank No 41202. The photo was taken during the Summer of 1963, a few days before the line closed. *Richard Greenhalgh*

North of Bridgnorth

The original Severn Valley Railway route never terminated at Bridgnorth, but ran through to Shrewsbury, 22½ miles to the north, via Coalport, Ironbridge and Buildwas. In recent years proposals have been put forward to extend the Severn Valley line the 10½ miles from Bridgnorth to Buildwas (Abbey), which would link the existing SVR with Ironbridge Gorge Museum sites and other attractions in the Coalbrookdale area.

For such a scheme to come to fruition, certain factors would need to be addressed:

The demolition of Ironbridge power station (one cooling tower in the way).

The rebuilding and stabilisation of railway earthworks in the Ironbridge gorge at Jackfield. The diversion of the railway formation immediately north of Bridgnorth tunnel – housing on the formation.

The lowering of a length of Hollybush Road in Bridgnorth to regain railway bridge clearance.

The co-operation of the local highway authority and several local landowners.

All of this would cost a lot of money, but would not be impossible.

In 1965 few people believed that trains would ever run again over the 16 miles from Bridgnorth to Kidderminster, but they now do. So, never say never…

ACKNOWLEDGEMENTS

Thanks for help in the compilation of this Visitor Guide are due to Tony Bending, Anthony Booth, Mick York and to Peter Townsend at Silver Link Publishing for layout and production .

Right: The interior of the purpose-built Retail Shop at **Kidderminster Town station.** Look for the sign 'Station Emporium' above the entrance door, which is situated on the right of the concourse if you enter from the Booking Hall. *SVR Archive*

THE RETAIL SHOPS

The shops on the Severn Valley Railway provide a valuable contribution to the Railway's income.

There are shops at **Kidderminster, Highley (The Engine House) and Bridgnorth.**

A varied range of specialist books, DVDs and magazines is available for the enthusiast, while for the modeller a range of train sets and accessories from various manufacturers, including Bachmann and Peco, are stocked.

A colourful range of Severn Valley Railway clothing can be purchased – fleece jackets, sweatshirts, T-shirts and hats are among the items available. For visitors looking for souvenirs of their visit to the railway, local-interest books, postcards, greetings cards, tea-towels, calendars, china, fridge magnets, key rings, and much more are on sale. For the younger visitor/enthusiast, an extensive selection of 'Thomas and Friends' merchandise, toys, books, playsets and individual models are stocked. SVR goods are also available online at svrshop.co.uk

Above: The Retail Shop at **The Engine House** visitor centre at **Highley** is located to the right just inside the main entrance. *SVR Archive*

Right: The Retail Shop at Bridgnorth station is seen here. *SVR Archive*

Above: Enjoying lunch in the GWR dining car of the Kidderminster-based 'Severn Valley Limited' train. . *Sharon Dredge*

Above: Time for desserts in the LMSR dining car of the Bridgnorth-based 'Severn Valley Venturer' train. *Chris Lewis*

On-Train Catering

Step back in time to the golden age of steam train travel! Dine in period style as the beautiful Worcestershire and Shropshire countryside slips past the window.

SVR steam-hauled dining services operate most weekends and on selected weekdays during the summer months.

For an experience that is certainly out of the ordinary, why not sample one of the Murder Mystery dining trains or maybe hire one of the beautifully restored observation saloons? The

saloons can be provided with a variety of food options and a steward to look after guests' every need throughout the day!

For that special celebration, a gathering with a difference or a business function that will certainly be a talking point for a very long time, look no further than dining trains on the Severn Valley Railway.

Most SVR trains, excluding dining services, provide a trolley service of hot and cold drinks and light snacks. Beers, wines and spirits are also available.

Below: the interior of one of the two GWR-designed Inspection Saloons on the SVR, now used as Observation/Refreshment Saloons in heritage service. *SVR Archive*

Below: The refreshment trolleys are popular, and in use along the corridors of many of our trains. *Bob Warwick*

Above: Service with a smile in 'The Engine House Cafe' at the SVR visitor centre at Highley. *SVR Archive*

Above: The cosy bar of 'The Railwayman's Arms' at Bridgnorth station. *Tony Bending*

OFF-TRAIN CATERING

Kidderminster: The King & Castle is popular with the locals, which tells you something! It serves a range of cask ales, along with hot and cold meals throughout the day. A Camra award winning pub.

The Refreshment Room is a comfortable licensed restaurant close to the station platforms. Good food and drink are available to eat in or take away for the whole family.

Bewdley: The Station Buffet serves hot and cold meals, snacks and beverages to eat in or take away.

Arley: The station kiosk offers a range of snacks and hot and cold drinks. at weekends and busy times.

Below: A period atmosphere pervades 'The King and Castle' public house that is enjoyed by both visitors and 'locals' alike. *Tony Bending*

Highley: The Engine House Café offers a wide selection of hot and cold meals to be enjoyed from one of the best country views on the railway.

Highley and Hampton Loade
The station kiosks offer a range of snacks and hot and cold drinks at weekends and busy times.

Bridgnorth: **The Railwayman's Arms**, right on the platform, is full of atmosphere, and a great place to meet for a glass or two from a selection of real ales. It is a regular Camra award winner.

The Refreshment Room serves hot and cold meals, snacks and beverages to eat in or take away. It is our newest catering establishment.

Below: 'The Refreshment Room' is a licensed restaurant adjacent to the Kidderminster Town concourse. Outside railway operating hours, it can be made available for conferences and event hire. *Tony Bending*

Above: Steam galas are usually held during one Spring and one extended Autumn weekend each year. The scene in Bridgnorth yard can be very busy, as depicted in this view on 7 October 2009. Visiting GWR 4-6-0 No 4936 *Kinlet Hall* raises steam, together with GWR 0-6-0 pannier tank No 5764, GWR 4-6-0 No 7802 *Bradley Manor* and LMSR Class 5 2-6-0 No 42968. *T. John Foster*

Rail Events

Below: The Diesel Gala is held on a May weekend each year. At Kidderminster on 21 May 2016, a large assembly of both historic and modern diesel locomotives is present, including Deltic, Western, Peak, Class 37 and Class 68 designs in this view. *Phil Bland*

ROAD VEHICLE EVENTS

A variety of special events occur on the Railway each year. This page shows those involving historic road vehicles, thus providing both rail and road transport nostalgia.

Left: The 'On the Buses' event is centred on Bewdley station car park, and is usually held during early September. Here is a fine group of some of the 20 buses gathered from different parts of Britain on 10 September 2017. *John Titlow*

Right: Here is a fine parade of cars opposite Highley station during the 'Classic Vehicle Day' on 30 July 2017. Similar line-ups can be found at other stations along the Railway during this event. *John Titlow*

Left: A recent addition to the SVR events list is 'Steam on the Road', usually held in mid-August. It features a variety of traction engines, road tractors, road rollers, etc, assembled around the Kidderminster Town station area. Here is the scene on 13 August 2016. *Scott Lewis*

Right: A gathering that is advertised locally is the meeting of 'mechanical horse' road lorries at Kidderminster every year. These charismatic vehicles were commonplace in railway cartage service until the early 1970s, and relatively few are preserved. Three that have been saved appear in this view on 12 May 2017. *John Giles*

THE SANTA EXPERIENCE...

Above: There is excitement on the platform at Arley station on 20 December 2015. SR 'Battle of Britain' 4-6-2 No 34053 *Sir Keith Park* is approaching with an empty train ready to transport visitors returning from Arley to Kidderminster after their visit to Santa's grotto. *John Oates*

Below: Earlier, an even more exciting moment occurred when children met Santa and received a present in his grotto at Arley. *Lewis Maddox*

...AND OTHER EVENTS

Right: 'Step Back to the 1940s' is an event usually held on two consecutive weekends in late June/ early July. SVR stations take part, with re-enactors performing, memorabilia displays, music concerts and a live battle. Here, a 1940's shop scene has been recreated on Kidderminster Town station concourse. *SVR Archive*

Left: 'Family Activities' take place at The Engine House at Highley during school holidays, all designed to keep the children entertained. A steam loco and Peppa Pig seem to be doing just that in this August 2016 scene. *SVR Archive*

Right: 'Ghost Trains' provide some seemingly unforgettable experiences during certain mid-week evenings in October. That is, if you dare to take a ride... the train Guard will provide reassurance of course... *SVR Archive*

Left: There is usually an 'Open House Weekend' at the start of the operating season in April of each year, when behind-the-scenes tours are arranged to some of our operating and engineering facilities. There are also model railway layouts installed at Kidderminster and Highley. *Keith Wilkinson*

RAILWAY STAFF

The Booking Clerk

The Station Staff

The Loco Driver and Fireman

On this page are shown some of the Staff that passengers are most likely to see on a visit to the Railway.

On the opposite page are shown a representative selection of the many people that might not be seen on a quick visit. But without them all, the SVR would be unable to function.

The Guard

The Ticket Inspector

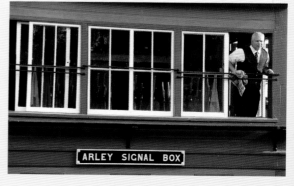

The Signalman

Civil Engineering

Permanent Way

Locomotive Repairs

Locomotive Maintenance

Carriage Restoration

Santa Support Team

Buffet Car Team

Junior Club

CIVIL ENGINEERING

Much of the major work of civil engineering is performed by contractors brought in for specific projects, but there remains plenty of work that is performed by SVR full-time and volunteer staff on appropriate jobs, bearing in mind safety considerations. The tunnel drainage project, of 2012 for instance, required contractors, SVR staff and volunteers to cooperate to complete the work at the end of a very short line closure period.

Victoria Bridge – new upper structure and shot blasting lower structure.

Bewdley tunnel – drainage clear-out and new track.

Highley – new footbridge.

Bewdley – attention to sandstone structure of Wribbenhall viaduct.

Arley – drainage clearance and new platform structure.

County boundary (Kinlet) – major earthworks including soil nailing of the embankment.

PERMANENT WAY

The Permanent Way Department is responsible for the track. This includes all maintenance, line inspection, hedging and fencing. A track-laying gang consisting of full-time and volunteer staff works out of Bridgnorth, with a further gang of volunteers based at Bewdley.

Hampton Loade – new track and pointwork.

Chelmarsh – drainage and new track.

SIGNALLING AND TELECOMMUNICATIONS

The Signal Department of the Severn Valley Railway is responsible for the operation of the most comprehensive signalling system on any preserved railway. There are seven signal boxes on the Railway, located at Kidderminster, Bewdley South, Bewdley North, Arley, Highley, Hampton Loade and Bridgnorth, and the total system comprises some 50 track circuits and 220 levers.

The IT Department is responsible for telecommunications on the SVR, and also for the provision and maintenance of the SVR's IT network, together with its associated hardware. Some specialist areas, such as accounts software and our network of EPOS tills, are managed by external suppliers.

Kidderminster – new signal gantry. *Tom Clarke*

Bewdley – pointwork alignment and linkage attention.

THE LISTING

Loco No	Class	Wheel Arrangement	Builder	Year built	Weight
Ex-Great Western Railway					
813	PTR	0-6-0ST	Hudswell Clarke, Leeds	1900	44 tons
1450	14XX	0-4-2T	Collett, Swindon	1935	41 tons
1501	15XX	0-6-0PT	Hawksworth, Swindon	1949	58 tons
2857	28XX	2-8-0	Churchward, Swindon	1918	115 tons
4150	51XX	2-6-2T	Churchward, Swindon	1947	78 tons
4566	45XX	2-6-2T	Churchward, Swindon	1924	57 tons
4930 *Hagley Hall*	'Hall'	4-6-0	Collett, Swindon	1929	121 tons
5164	51XX	2-6-2T	Churchward, Swindon	1930	78 tons
5764	57XX	0-6-0PT	Collett, Swindon	1929	47 tons
7325 (or 9303)	43XX	2-6-0	Collett, Swindon	1932	105 tons
7714	57XX	0-6-0PT	Collett, Stoke-on-Trent	1930	47 tons
7802 *Bradley Manor*	'Manor'	4-6-0	Collett, Swindon	1938	109 tons
7812 *Erlestoke Manor*	'Manor'	4-6-0	Collett, Swindon	1939	109 tons
7819 *Hinton Manor*	'Manor'	4-6-0	Collett, Swindon	1939	109 tons
Ex-Southern Railway (rebuilt by British Railways)					
34027 *Taw Valley*	'West Country'	4-6-2	Bulleid, Brighton	1946	139 tons
Ex- London Midland & Scottish Railway					
42968	6P5F	2-6-0	Stanier, Crewe	1934	111 tons
43106	4MT	2-6-0	Ivatt, Darlington	1951	99 tons
45110 *R.A.F. Biggin Hill*	5MT	4-6-0	Stanier, Vulcan	1935	124 tons
46443	2MT	2-6-0	Ivatt, Crewe	1950	84 tons
47383	3F	0-6-0T	Fowler, Vulcan	1926	49 tons
48773 (or 8233)	8F	2-8-0	Stanier, Glasgow	1940	126 tons
Ex-British Railways					
75069	4MT	4-6-0	Riddles, Swindon	1955	119 tons
80079	4MT	2-6-4T	Riddles, Brighton	1954	86 tons
Ex-Army					
600 Gordon	WD	2-10-0	Riddles, Glasgow	1943	134 tons
Ex-Industrial					
686 *The Lady Armaghdale*		0-6-0T	Leeds	1898	35 tons
2047 *Warwickshire*		0-6-0ST	Leeds	1926	30 tons

FURTHER READING...

If you would like to learn more about the Severn Valley Railway, the following books are available while stocks last from the SVR shops shown on page 49. Please note that the prices quoted are correct a May 2018.

Severn Valley Railway Recollections John Stretton, Silver Link Publishing, £6.00
Heritage Rly Guide-The Severn Valley Railway Michael Vanns, Pen & Sword, £19.99
Past & Present-The Severn Valley Railway Vol 1 Roger Siviter, Silver Link Publishing, £15.99
Past & Present-The Severn Valley Railway Vol 2 John Stretton, Silver Link Publishing, £19.99
Severn Valley Railway-A View from the Past Michael Vanns, Shrewdale Publishing, £15.00
The story of The Big Flood Phil Sowden, Silver Link Publishing, £6.00
Country Railway Routes- Kidderminster to Shrewsbury Middleton Press, £18.95
Severn Valley Railway Journey David C.Williams, Silver Link Publishing, £20.00

THE PHOTOGRAPHS

Here are SVR-based steam locomotives which are either on display at The Engine House visitor centre at Highley or under repair at Bridgnorth. Others in the fleet are illustrated throughout the pages of this Guide.

No 600 at Bridgnorth. *David Idle*

No 7819 at Bridgnorth. *Duncan Ballard*

No 80079 at Arley. *David C. Williams*

No 2047 at Bridgnorth. *David Idle*

No 686 at Highley. *Nigel Cripps*

Please note that the listing of steam locomotives on the opposite page and diesels on the next page are made up of locomotives normally based on the SVR at the time of writing. However, throughout the year additional visiting locomotives are often to be seen on the Railway.

Locomotives from the SVR also visit other locations for galas, events or overhaul.

Historic diesel locomotives are used on the Severn Valley Railway to pull passenger trains in ordinary service and during special enthusiast events, also engineers' trains and for shunting duties.

Loco No	Class	Wheel Arrangement	Builder	Year built	Weight
Ex-British Railways					
(D431) 50 031 *Hood*	DE	Co-Co	Newton-le-Willows	1968	117 tons
(D435) 50 035 *Ark Royal*	DE	Co-Co	Newton-le-Willows	1968	117 tons
D444 (50 044) *Exeter*	DE	Co-Co	Newton-le-Willows	1968	117 tons
(D449) 50 049 *Defiance*	DE	Co-Co	Newton-le-Willows	1968	117 tons
D821 *Greyhound*	DH	B-B	Swindon	1960	79 tons
D1013 *Western Ranger*	DH	C-C	Swindon	1962	109 tons
D1062 *Western Courier*	DH	C-C	Crewe	1963	109 tons
D3022 (08 015)	DE	0-6-0	Derby	1953	49 tons
D3201 (08 133)	DE	0-6-0	Derby	1955	49 tons
D3586 (08 471)	DE	0-6-0	Crewe	1974	49 tons
D3802 (08 635)	DE	0-6-0	Crewe	1974	49 tons
D4100 (09 012) *Dick Hardy*	DE	0-6-0	Horwich	1961	49 tons
D4103 (08 845, 09 107)	DE	0-6-0	Horwich	1961	49 tons
D4126 (08 896) *Stephen Dent*	DE	0-6-0	Horwich	1962	49 tons
12099 (class 11)	DE	0-6-0	Derby	1952	49 tons
D5410 (27 059, 27 205)	DE	Bo-Bo	Smethwick	1962	77 tons
D7029	DH	B-B	Manchester	1962	74 tons
D9551 *Angus*	DH	0-6-0	Swindon	1965	50 tons
Ex-Industrial Locos					
D2957 (319290)	DM	0-4-0	Lincoln	1953	28 tons
D2960 *Silver Spoon* (281269)	DM	0-4-0	Lincoln	1950	28 tons
D2961 (418596)	DE	0-4-0	Lincoln	1957	28 tons
DH = Diesel hydraulic DM = Diesel mechanical DE = Diesel electric					

No D9551 at Bridgnorth. *David Bissett*

No D2960 at Kidderminster. *Tim Davis*

No 12099 at Kidderminster. *John Whitehouse*

No D3022 at Bewdley. *David C. Williams*

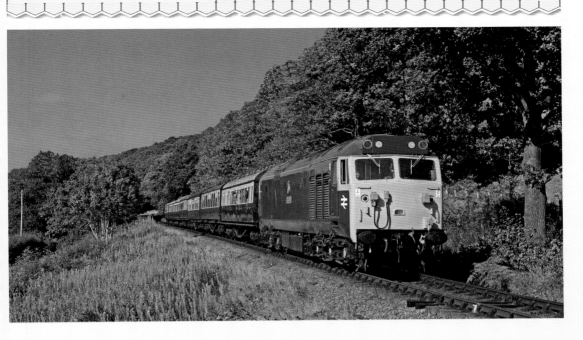

Above: Four BR Class 50 diesel-electric locomotives of the Co-Co wheel arrangement have been based on the SVR at Kidderminster for many years. These operate in the valley, on the main line and also visit heritage railway events elsewhere via Network Rail. In idyllic weather conditions at the Diesel Gala on 1 October 2015, No 50 035 *Ark Royal* has just passed Northwood with a Bridgnorth to Kidderminster train. *Malcolm Ranieri*

Below: The SVR is host to five diesel multiple unit (dmu) cars, all being of 'Derby lightweight' design, built there between 1959 and 1961, and latterly designated as BR Class 108. These cars sometimes run separately in 3-car and 2-car formations, but often combine to produce a 5-car set, as here. The full set is seen leaving Bewdley tunnel with a Festive Season Kidderminster to Bridgnorth service on 28 December 2016. *Malcolm Ranieri*

THE PASSENGER COACHES

The SVR has arguably the largest collection of historic coaches in Britain, with over 60 working vehicles, dating from 1912 to 1963. They have been purchased and restored to original condition and livery by enthusiastic volunteers, initially often in the open air, and independently of the SVR. The same people also raised the necessary funds, which in some cases approached £200,000. Here are the original railways and liveries you will see on this line.

Above: **Great Western, 1838-1947**
Covered London Paddington to the South West, Wales and south Merseyside. Oldest of the main line companies. Brunel was its famous engineer. The SVR has two sets of GWR coaches in 'chocolate-and-cream' livery This is Brake Third Open 650 of 1940. *David A . Smith*

Left: **London, Midland and Scottish, 1923-1947**
From London Euston and St Pancras, served the Midlands, Wales, North West England and Scotland, amalgamating many earlier companies. The SVR uniquely has a complete working LMSR train in 'crimson lake' livery. This is Restaurant First Open No 7511 of 1934. *Mick Flint*

Right: **London and North Eastern, 1923-1947**
From London Kings Cross, Liverpool Street and Marylebone to East Anglia, East Midlands, North East England and Scotland, also amalgamating many earlier companies. The SVR runs the longest complete working LNER train in 'varnished teak' livery. This is Kitchen Composite No 7960 of 1936. *David Dawson*

Left: **British Railways, 1948-1997**
Formed at nationalisation of Britain's four main line railways, BR developed new designs based on the best of its predecessors. SVR has examples from the 1950s and early 1960s, some in the earlier carmine-and-cream livery, some in later maroon livery. This is Corridor Composite No 16202 of 1961. *David Dawson*

THE GOODS VEHICLES

Above: The Railway operates a demonstration freight train at most steam galas and other special occasions. This is Chelmarsh, north of Hampton Loade, on 30 March 2012. The wagons have been bought by volunteer effort and restored by volunteers in the Wagon Department at Bewdley. The result, as seen here, is a very credible GWR goods train headed appropriately by GWR 2-8-0 No 2857, which spent 46 years in main line freight service before the preservation era. *Alan Corfield*

Left: An earlier outing for the demonstration freight train occurred on Monday 26 February 1996 GWR 0-6-0 pannier tank No 7714 provided the power, and is seen here on the climb from Victoria Bridge to Arley station.
Malcolm Ranieri

SEVERN VALLEY FAVOURITES

Right: Great Western Railway Collett 4-6-0 No 4930 *Hagley Hall* assaults the climb from Victoria Bridge to Arley station with the northbound 'Severn Valley Limited' dining train formed of GWR coaches on 23 September 1984. *Bob Green*

Left: London, Midland and Scottish Railway Stanier Class 5 4-6-0 No 5110, here seen as BR No 45110, leads a rake of BR Mark 1 coaches in carmine-and-cream livery along the straight section north of Hampton Loade on 22 March 2008, bound for Bridgnorth. *Dave Sanders*

Right: British Railways Standard Class 4 4-6-0 No 75069 leaves Northwood for Bewdley with the 'Severn Valley Limited' dining train from Bridgnorth to Kidderminster on 25 March 1990. *David C. Williams*

Great Western Railway Collett 2-6-0 No 7325 makes a vigorous ascent of the 1 in 100 of Eardington bank with a photographers' charter special train on 9 November 1998. *Bob Green*

THE SEVERN VALLEY RAILWAY COMPANIES

The Severn Valley Railway's purpose is to 'preserve, maintain and operate the SVR as a working museum of railway history for the education and enjoyment of present and future generations'. It is a leading heritage railway carrying some 250,000 visitors each year. Operated by over 1,700 working volunteers who give up their time to restore and run heritage trains and maintain the historic infrastructure, it is supported by approximately 80 full-time equivalent staff. The whole provides visitors with a memorable experience of the golden age of rail travel.

'Severn Valley Railway' is an umbrella name for three constituent organisations, summarised as follows; -

Severn Valley Railway (Holdings) Plc is a share capital company. No monetry dividend is paid to shareholders, almost 14,000 in number, and all profits are used to support the running of the Railway. It owns the infrastructure and assets of the SVR, employs the paid staff, and is responsible for the operation, finance, governance, planning, customer service and management of the SVR.

Severn Valley Railway Company Limited is a company limited by guarantee, and has a membership of over 12,000. Approximately 1,700 of these members are actively involved as volunteers, helping to run the SVR. In 1970 the company succeeded the original Severn Valley Railway Society, and bought the first part of line, from Bridgnorth to Hampton Loade, shortly afterwards. Ownership of the line passed to the Holdings company in 1972, although the SVR Company Limited remains as the membership and volunteer organisation and is a very active supporting body. Its large membership enables it to give a great deal of financial help to the Railway, supporting or wholly funding projects which might not otherwise be possible.

Severn Valley Railway Charitable Trust Limited, which changed its name from SVR Rolling Stock Trust Company in mid-2012, was incorporated and registered as a company limited by guarantee in late 2001, and was registered with the Charity Commission in mid-2002. It owns some of the rolling stock used on the SVR, and employs paid staff and volunteers. The Trust has objectives embracing preservation and restoration of infrastructure and rolling stock and, where appropriate, the timely acquisition and thus the safeguarding of rolling stock. It seeks to educate the public in its work and provides support for heritage skills training.

The scene on 24 May 1970, with a busy Bridgnorth station viewed from Pan Pudding Hill. LMSR Stanier Class 8F 2-8-0 No 8233 (BR No 48773) is about to depart from Platform 1 for Hampton Loade and LMR Ivatt Class 4 2-6-0 No 43106 is entering the loco yard. This is the second day of passenger timetable operation in preservation, the weather contrasting with the dreariness of the first day. *Derek Jones*

SEVERN VALLEY RAILWAY COMPANY MEMBERSHIP

Become a supporter of the Railway!

By joining the Severn Valley Railway Company Limited as a member, you can look forward to a range of exclusive benefits, including reduced fares, special events and the quarterly 'SVR News' magazine, all for an affordable membership fee. This Company is the supporting body of the Railway, attracting volunteers from its 12,000 plus membership to help operate the line.

To find out more please visit www.svr.co.uk, where you can also join online if you wish, or email membership@svrlive.com.

Alternatively, please contact the Membership Secretary, Severn Valley Railway Co. Ltd., Number One, Comberton Hill, Kidderminster, Worcestershire DY10 1QR. (telephone 01562 757930 (Mondays to Wednesdays, 9am to 2pm)

Would you like to help us operate the Railway?

As a Member, you could also help us run the Railway. We have a wide range of volunteer opportunities throughout the Railway – you will be surprised at the variety of jobs needed to deliver that unique SVR experience. We couldn't run the Railway without volunteers; they are the lifeblood of the line and you too could become a valued member of the team. There is often great camaraderie and new friends have been made through shared SVR experiences.

Why not take a look at the volunteer website www.svr-vlo.org.uk which provides information on the volunteering opportunities available. Interested? Then complete the 'contact us' form or call the Volunteer Liaison Office on 01299 401776 (with voicemail) or email vlo@svrlive.com The office at Bewdley Station is open during most Tuesdays and Thursdays, also on some weekends.

Falling Sands Viaduct, on the outskirts of Kidderminster, is the subject of an appeal by the SVR Charitable Trust to raise funds for the restoration of the 1870s-built structure, to commence in 2019. In this view, it is being crossed by GWR 4-6-0 No 6023 *King Edward II* at the head of a Bridgnorth-bound train on 21 April 2018. *Ralph Ward*

Why does the SVR need a Charitable Trust?

This is something many people ask, especially when the Railway takes in a healthy income from ticket sales, and from its shops, cafes and pubs. The fact is that while this income does indeed cover the day-to-day running costs of the Railway, a great deal more funding is needed to pay for the immense and never-ending task of maintaining and restoring the SVR's extensive rolling stock, infrastructure and permanent way. This is precisely why the SVR Charitable Trust was created in 2012; to help fund restoration and maintenance projects, to help arrest the decline of heritage engineering skills and to safeguard the long-term future and operational capability of the Railway.

It's easy to make a donation online at svrtrust.org.uk, or just ask for a donation leaflet at one of the SVR's ticket offices.

01562 757940
fundraising@svrtrust.org.uk

How is the Charitable Trust helping the Railway?

• In 2018, in partnership with SVR Holdings plc, the Trust launched an appeal to restore Falling Sands Viaduct. The Railway must raise £275,000 towards the overall cost, and as this publication goes to press, we hope that our bid to the Heritage Lottery Fund for the remaining £1 million will succeed.

• The Trust supports many other projects; locomotive, carriage and wagon restorations are among these, as are a number of infrastructure projects. It has secured funding to improve the SVR's wheelchair accessibility and will contribute significantly to developments at Bridgnorth station, including the installation of a turntable.

• The Charitable Trust is working towards a £10 million balance for its endowment Futures Fund, with the pot reaching £1,200,000 in spring 2018. Income from this endowment will allow sustainable investment on the Railway in the years to come.

• It is the majority funder for the SVR's Heritage Skills Training Academy, in which apprentices are acquiring essential engineering skills to keep the Railway in good shape for the future.

LOTTERY FUNDED

BEWDLEY: A wintry scene across the Georgian-era rooftops of Bewdley; LMSR Stanier Class 5 2-6-0 No 42968 departs for Bridgnorth on 8 December 2012, whilst a Kidderminster train leaves simultaneously. St Anne's church stands sentinel on the right, and the Clent Hills are visible on the left horizon. *Alan Corfield*

Here is a gathering of one hundred long-served SVR volunteer members who travelled on the special train commemorating the fiftieth anniversary of the founding of the preservation scheme on 6 July 2015. The backdrop consists of five steam locomotives specially assembled in Bridgnorth Loco Yard. *Bob Sweet*

FIFTY YEARS OF ENDEAVOUR

The Severn Valley Railway Society was the forerunner of the Severn Valley Railway Company. Its first meeting was held at Kidderminster on 6th July 1965. Within a few days, its first severe test was to halt the demolition of Bridgnorth station, and this was successfully achieved with a mixture of determination and good luck. Had this not happened, there would be no railway at Bridgnorth today.

All of the people present in the scene above had just enjoyed a journey on the 50th Anniversary special train from Kidderminster, organised to celebrate the momentous achievements of half-a-century of dedicated effort. These members were drawn from many walks of life, but all had the common aim of reviving the Severn Valley Railway, using appropriate experience, whether it was in legal, financial, engineering, operating or commercial matters. Or simply ready and willing to put in some darned hard work!

Success was not guaranteed however; early on, there were many doubters, including some railway people who might have been expected to give the new project a chance. But dogged determination won through, and today the Railway has made the sight and sound of steam trains travelling along this picturesque part of the Severn Valley a commonplace event.

It is impossible to determine accurately what the next half-century will bring, but certainly the Severn Valley Railway will hope to play its part. At present, the activities of the Railway continue to bring great pleasure to the many people who visit the line. This can take the form of dining in style on the trains, or by simply soaking up the atmosphere of a bygone era from a station seat! And there are so many other enjoyable experiences on the Railway.

This brief Visitor Guide can only touch upon the surface of the Railway's work, but we hope that it will serve either to whet your appetite if you have yet to make a visit, or to provide you with a reminder in text and picture of a previous pleasurable encounter. Or, last but certainly not least, provide a useful Guide for…today!